THIRD TIME'S A CHARM

21 Colorful Options for Charm-Pack Quilts

Barbara Groves and Mary Jacobson

OF ME AND MY SISTER DESIGNS

Martingale®

Create with Confidence

Third Time's a Charm: 21 Colorful Options for Charm-Pack Quilts
© 2019 by Barbara Groves and Mary Jacobson

Martingale®
19021 120th Ave. NE, Ste. 102
Bothell, WA 98011-9511 USA
ShopMartingale.com

Printed in China
24 23 22 21 20 19   8 7 6 5 4 3 2 1

Library of Congress Cataloging-in-Publication Data
is available upon request.

ISBN: 978-1-68356-026-5

MISSION STATEMENT

We empower makers who use fabric and yarn
to make life more enjoyable.

CREDITS

PUBLISHER AND
CHIEF VISIONARY OFFICER
Jennifer Erbe Keltner

CONTENT DIRECTOR
Karen Costello Soltys

DESIGN MANAGER
Adrienne Smitke

MANAGING EDITOR
Tina Cook

PRODUCTION MANAGER
Regina Girard

ACQUISITIONS AND
DEVELOPMENT EDITOR
Laurie Baker

BOOK AND
COVER DESIGNER
Mia Mar

TECHNICAL EDITOR
Ellen Pahl

PHOTOGRAPHER
Brent Kane

COPY EDITOR
Ariel Anderson

ILLUSTRATOR
Sandy Loi

CONTENTS

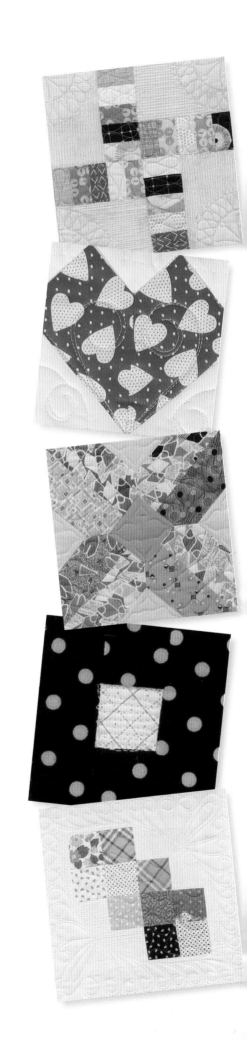

INTRODUCTION

We love precuts and always have! Our love affair with precuts began when we were shop owners way back in the '90s. Quilting was booming, and many new and exciting things were happening—like precuts! This was before the fabric companies were cutting and assembling them directly from the mills, so shop owners had to cut their own. We would sometimes order two sets of a collection and cut one entire set into bundles of precuts! Let's just say there were many late-night cutting parties that lasted into the wee hours of the morning. We also went through yards and yards of colorful ribbons for tying bundles.

So, what is a precut? It's a collection of fabrics that are cut to a specific size or shape. Since they're from the same line of fabric, they will all work well together. As shop owners, we started out cutting fat quarters, 18" × 21" pieces, because they were best sellers. Charm squares, 5" squares of fabric, quickly became the second most desired option. We had a brown-bag kit filled with charm squares ready to sew into a fast quilt. It was very popular—shake, grab, and sew!

Fast-forward to today and the modern precut. Fabric companies have made it so easy for us! Precuts can be ordered when a shop owner first views a new fabric collection. Precuts typically arrive in the shops a few weeks before a fabric collection ships. This probably started out as a way for shop owners to get a sample quilt finished and hung before the bolts of the collection arrived. Now we just expect those cute packets of fabric to arrive like clockwork to tantalize and inspire us!

When we owned our quilt shop, we noticed that our customers would walk through the door and head straight to the stacks of precuts. Almost every packet was touched, loved, and admired. The inevitable question came shortly after: "What do I do with these?"

The answer to that question is what led to our business today. We had to start designing ways to use precuts. We would hand out a free pattern when a customer purchased a precut packet. Our first charm book was a collection of those patterns.

Through the years, we've continued designing patterns that use precuts, and we still love using them. We can't say that we have a favorite precut because it's always the one currently in our hands!

This is our third book on charm squares, and in the tradition of the first two books, the quilts have been named after some of our favorite girls. Book one started with Amanda and Bertha. The quilts are presented in alphabetical order, and in this book, they begin with Olivia. We also made three quilts with every pattern in very different fabrics to show versatility and provide inspiration. Sometimes it's difficult imagining a quilt in different fabrics. We took the extra step to show other possibilities. Most of these quilts can be made in a day or a weekend by an experienced quilter. But they're easy enough for beginners to make quickly, too.

Enjoy these patterns using precut charm squares!

Barb   Mary

THE CHARM OF CHARM SQUARES

If you're wondering exactly what a charm square is, it's a 5" square of fabric. A charm pack is a bundle of 42 squares, 5" × 5", cut from one entire fabric collection. We love these bundles of joy because they allow us to own a square of everything in a fabric collection at an affordable price. We already know that the designer has done all the hard work of coordinating the fabrics.

Our number one tip regarding charm packs is to find one that you love. After that, anything is possible! Once you have a charm pack (and this book), the rest is easy!

That being said, though, not all charm packs are created equal. If a fabric collection is small, especially if it's a holiday-themed collection, you may receive a few repeats of some of the fabrics. Most often, they will all be different, at least in color. After we open a charm pack, we may find there's a fabric we don't really like or there aren't enough lights or darks for the project we're making. This is when we substitute one or two squares here and there. Not every charm pack works for every project, so helping it along is not breaking any rules!

When we select a charm pack for a quilt, we often purchase the backing and binding fabrics at the same time. We'll get a few extra inches of those fabrics to use in the quilt top. That way, if there's a fabric in the charm pack that we don't like or think doesn't work in the pattern we've chosen, we substitute it with some pieces of the binding or backing fabrics.

If it seems like there are too many lights or too many darks in a charm pack, or you're worried that not all of the charm squares will show up against the background, sort through the squares before sewing. While looking at the quilt diagram, pair or group the squares so that there's an even number of lights and darks. For Sarah on page 31, we placed the light squares in the center of the groupings so that they wouldn't be directly next to the white background. We use lots of white backgrounds in our quilts, but don't be afraid to use some color in yours.

You can always make these small quilts bigger. Ursula on page 43 is a great example of a quilt that begs to be made larger. To ramp up the size of a quilt, purchase additional (and different) charm packs from the same designer, and you'll be able to make more blocks for an instant scrappy quilt. If you purchase four times as many charm packs, you'll be able to make four times as many blocks.

BARB AND MARY'S TIPS FOR CHARMS

Below are a few tips and some tricks we use when working with charm packs.

* Use binding clips to keep like pieces together and organized while sewing and pressing.

* Cut and measure from the outer tip of the pinked edges. Whenever possible, we slice off the tiniest sliver of the pinked edge before cutting the pieces from the charm square. This isn't always possible, so check the individual pattern cutting diagrams carefully first to see if this will work.

* Don't be afraid to substitute or include a few 5" squares from your stash into the mix to add interest!

* Measure and trim your blocks before assembling. It only takes a few extra minutes, and you'll love the results! Sometimes we trim off only a few threads, but those blocks just seem to slide together afterward.

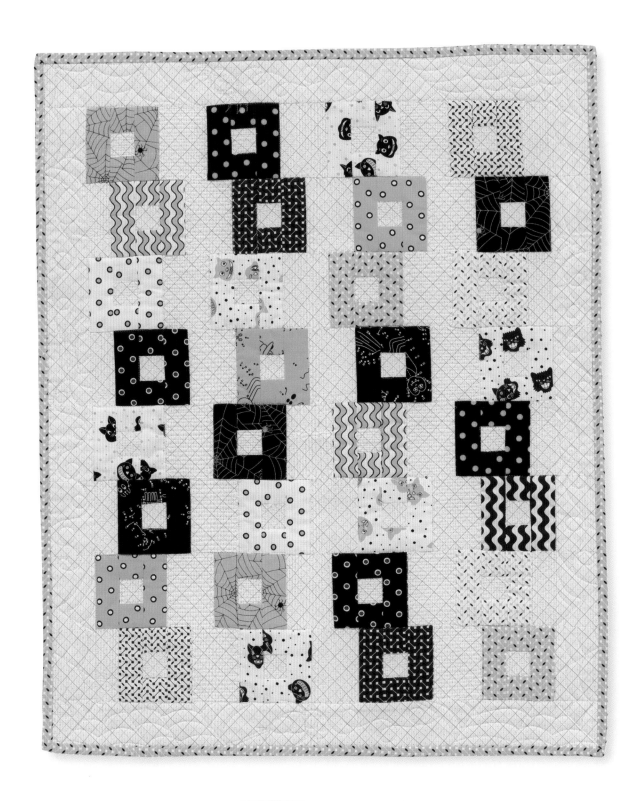

Finished quilt: 23½" × 28½"
Finished block: 3" × 3"

Third Time's a Charm

OLIVIA

You'll need only 32 charm squares for this cutie, so choose your favorites! A perfect pattern for seasonal or holiday quilts, Olivia can easily be used as a table topper. This version, sewn in Halloween prints, begs for some mini pumpkins, white gourds, and a bowl of candy corn.

MATERIALS

Yardage is based on 42"-wide fabric. Fabrics are from Dot Dot Boo by Me and My Sister Designs for Moda Fabrics.

- 32 charm squares, 5" × 5", of assorted prints for blocks*
- ⅝ yard of solid or print for block centers, setting blocks, and border
- ¼ yard of fabric for binding
- 1 yard of fabric for backing
- 28" × 33" piece of batting

*Moda charm packs contain 42 squares, 5" × 5".

CUTTING

Refer to the cutting guide for charm squares below, and keep like prints together.

From _each_ charm square, cut:

2 rectangles, 1½" × 3½"

2 squares, 1½" × 1½"

From the solid or print, cut:

2 strips, 1½" × 42"; crosscut into 32 squares, 1½" × 1½"

3 strips, 3½" × 42"; crosscut into:
- 32 rectangles, 2½" × 3½"
- 8 squares, 3½" × 3½"

2 strips, 2½" × 23½"

From the binding fabric, cut:

3 strips, 2¼" × 42"

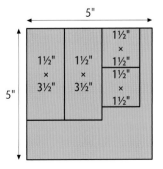

Cutting guide

MAKING THE BLOCKS

Use a ¼" seam allowance and short stitch length throughout. Press all seam allowances open.

1 For each block, choose:
- A matching set of 2 print 1½" squares and 2 print 1½" × 3½" rectangles
- 1 solid or print 1½" square

2 Sew the matching print squares to the top and bottom of the solid or print 1½" square. Sew the print rectangles to opposite sides of the unit to complete a block that measures 3½" square, including seam allowances. Make 32 blocks.

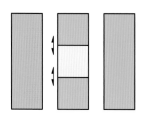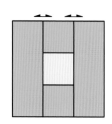

Make 32 blocks,
3½" × 3½".

ASSEMBLING THE QUILT

1 Arrange and sew four solid or print 2½" × 3½" rectangles, four pieced blocks, and one solid or print 3½" square as shown to make a row that measures 3½" × 23½". Make eight rows.

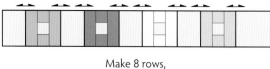

Make 8 rows,
3½" × 23½".

2 Lay out the rows, beginning with a row that starts with a rectangle on the left. Rotate every other row to start with a square.

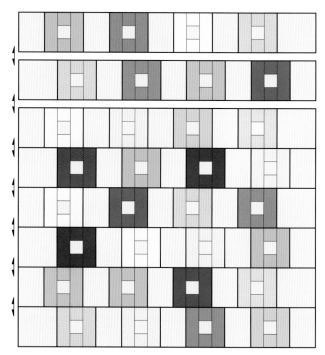

Quilt assembly

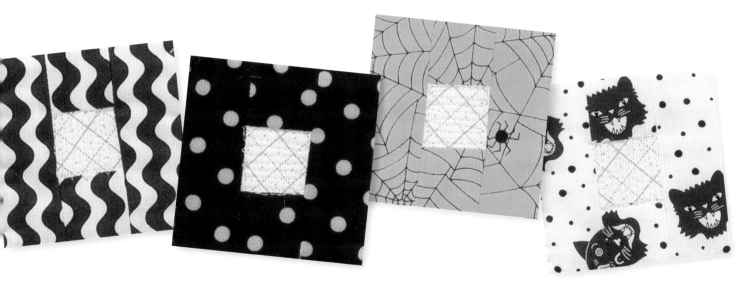

3 Join the rows to make the quilt center, which should measure 23½" × 24½", including seam allowances.

4 Sew the top and bottom borders to the quilt center. The quilt top should measure 23½" × 28½".

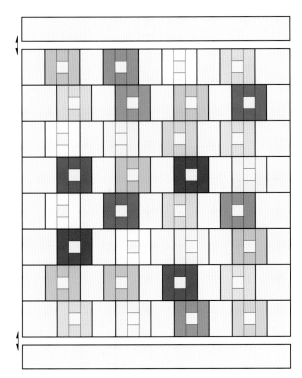

Adding borders

FINISHING

For more help on any of the finishing steps, go to ShopMartingale.com/HowtoQuilt for free downloadable information.

1 Layer and baste the quilt top, batting, and backing fabric.

2 Hand or machine quilt. The quilt shown is machine quilted with spiders, spider webs, and loops in the borders, with outline quilting around the inner and outer edges of the print squares, and with closely spaced straight lines in the background.

3 Use the 2¼" strips to make double-fold binding. Trim the excess batting and backing fabric and then attach the binding to the quilt.

Make a spring or summer quilt with a sky-blue background and floral prints like these from Cheeky by Urban Chiks.

Fabrics from On Meadowlark Pond by Kansas Troubles Quilters create a warm, earthy quilt with vintage appeal.

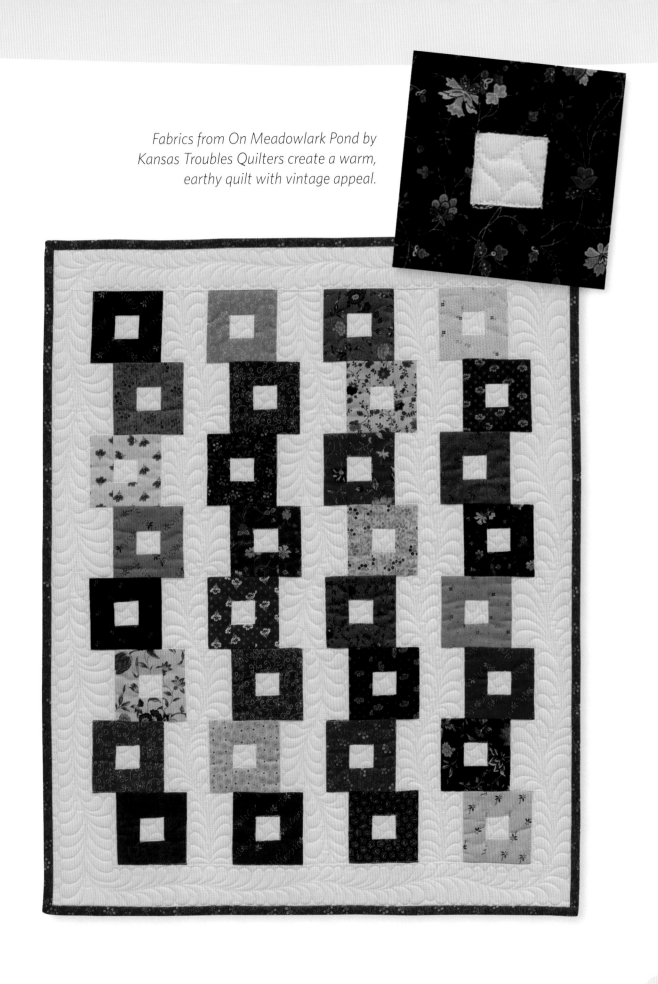

Olivia

Finished quilt: 28½" × 34½"
Finished block: 6" × 6"

POPPY

Whether you call these blocks Churn Dash or Shoo Fly, they're fun and simple to coordinate when using a charm pack. Ours is reminiscent of the colors and prints of fabrics from the 1930s—always cheerful and charming when set against a white background. Bet you can't make just one!

MATERIALS

Yardage is based on 42"-wide fabric. Fabrics are from Badda Bing by Me and My Sister Designs for Moda Fabrics.

- 40 charm squares, 5" × 5", of assorted prints for blocks*
- ⅞ yard of solid fabric for blocks
- ⅜ yard of print for border
- ⅓ yard of fabric for binding
- 1 yard of fabric for backing
- 33" × 39" piece of batting

Moda charm packs contain 42 squares, 5" × 5".

CUTTING

Refer to the cutting guide for charm squares, right, and keep like prints together.

From *each* charm square, cut:

1 square, 3" × 3"

4 squares, 1½" × 1½"

From the solid fabric, cut:

4 strips, 3" × 42"; crosscut into 40 squares, 3" × 3"

5 strips, 2½" × 42"; crosscut into:
- 20 squares, 2½" × 2½"
- 80 rectangles, 1½" × 2½"

From the border fabric, cut:

4 strips, 2½" × 42"; crosscut into:
- 2 strips, 2½" × 30½"
- 2 strips, 2½" × 28½"

From the binding fabric, cut:

4 strips, 2¼" × 42"

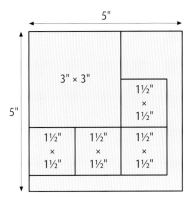

Cutting guide

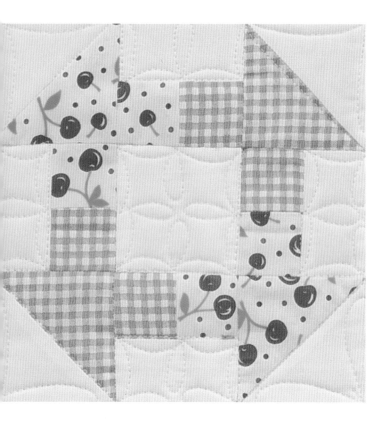

3 Select the prints for each block. You'll need a matching set of two half-square-triangle units and four 1½" squares from each of two prints. From the solid you'll need four 1½" × 2½" rectangles and one 2½" square.

4 Sew the contrasting print squares together in pairs. Make four units that measure 1½" × 2½", including seam allowances.

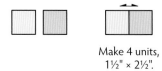

Make 4 units,
1½" × 2½".

5 Sew a solid 1½" × 2½" rectangle to each unit from step 4, arranging the two different prints as shown. Make four units that measure 2½" square, including seam allowances.

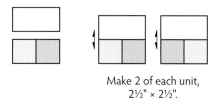

Make 2 of each unit,
2½" × 2½".

MAKING THE BLOCKS

Use a ¼" seam allowance and short stitch length throughout. Press all seam allowances open.

1 Draw a diagonal line from corner to corner on the wrong side of the solid 3" squares.

2 With right sides facing, layer a marked solid square with a 3" print square. Stitch ¼" from each side of the marked line. Cut along the line and press open to make two half-square-triangle units. Trim the units to measure 2½" square. Make a total of 80 units and keep like units together.

Make 80 units,
2½" × 2½".

6 Arrange and sew the units from steps 2 and 5 together in rows with the solid 2½" square as shown. Sew the rows together to complete a block that measures 6½" square, including seam allowances. Make 20 blocks.

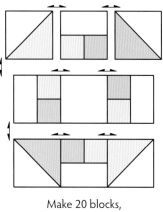

Make 20 blocks,
6½" × 6½".

ASSEMBLING THE QUILT

1 Sew four blocks together to make a row that measures 6½" × 24½", including seam allowances. Make five rows.

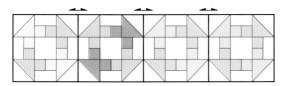

Make 5 rows,
6½" × 24½".

2 Join the rows to make the quilt center, which should measure 24½" × 30½", including seam allowances.

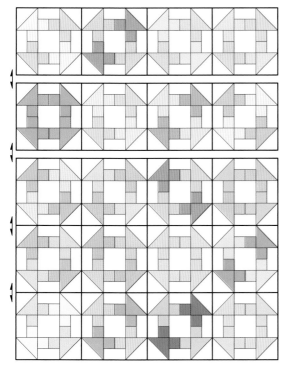

Quilt assembly

3 Sew a 30½"-long border strip to each side of the quilt center. Sew the 28½"-long strips to the top and bottom of the quilt center. The completed quilt top should measure 28½" × 34½".

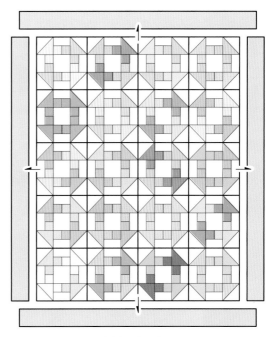

Adding borders

FINISHING

For more help on any of the finishing steps, go to ShopMartingale.com/HowtoQuilt for free downloadable information.

1 Layer and baste the quilt top, batting, and backing fabric.

2 Hand or machine quilt. The quilt shown is machine quilted with swags in the borders and with loops in the white background. Each Churn Dash is quilted in the ditch.

3 Use the 2¼" strips to make double-fold binding. Trim the excess batting and backing fabric and then attach the binding to the quilt.

Turn Poppy into a patriotic powerhouse using Star and Stripe Gatherings fabric by Primitive Gatherings.

Fabrics from Strawberry Jam by Corey Yoder add sparkle with Churn Dash corners that disappear and reappear at random against a medium solid background.

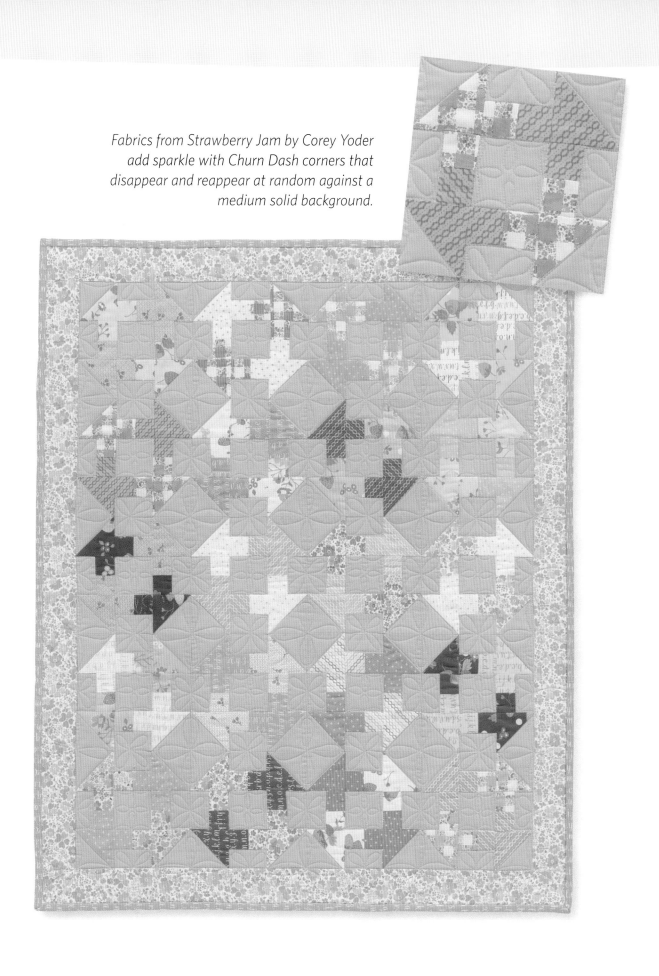

Finished quilt: 40½" × 46½"
Finished block: 6" × 6"

QUINN

We think this is the easiest quilt in the book. This is the quilt to make when you absolutely adore a specific collection. There's very little cutting, and you can take advantage of all 5" of every square in the charm pack. If you hate leftovers, you'll love this quilt!

MATERIALS

Yardage is based on 42"-wide fabric. Fabrics are from Chantilly by Fig Tree & Co. for Moda Fabrics.

- 42 charm squares, 5" × 5", of assorted prints for blocks*
- 1¼ yards of solid for blocks and border
- ⅜ yard of fabric for binding
- 3 yards of fabric for backing
- 47" × 53" piece of batting

Moda charm packs contain 42 squares, 5"×5".

CUTTING

From the solid fabric, cut:

13 strips, 2" × 42"; crosscut into:
- 42 rectangles, 2" × 5"
- 42 rectangles, 2" × 6½"

5 strips, 2½" × 42"

From the binding fabric, cut:

5 strips, 2¼" × 42"

MAKING THE BLOCKS

Use a ¼" seam allowance and short stitch length throughout. Press all seam allowances open.

Sew a solid 2" × 5" rectangle to the bottom of each charm square. Sew a solid 2" × 6½" rectangle to the left edge of the squares to complete a block that measures 6½" square, including seam allowances. Make 42 blocks.

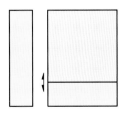 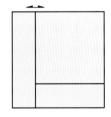

Make 42 blocks,
6½" × 6½".

ASSEMBLING THE QUILT

1. Arrange and sew six blocks into a row, rotating them as shown. Make four rows that measure 6½" × 36½", including seam allowances.

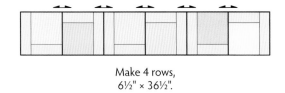

Make 4 rows,
6½" × 36½".

2. Arrange and sew six blocks into a row, rotating them as shown. Make three rows that measure 6½" × 36½", including seam allowances.

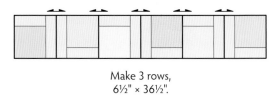

Make 3 rows,
6½" × 36½".

3. Lay out the rows, alternating them as shown. Join the rows to make the quilt center, which should measure 36½" × 42½", including seam allowances.

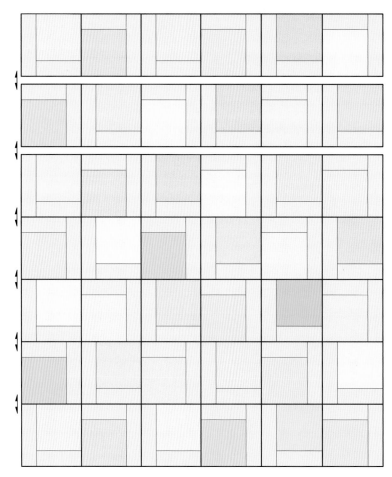

Quilt assembly

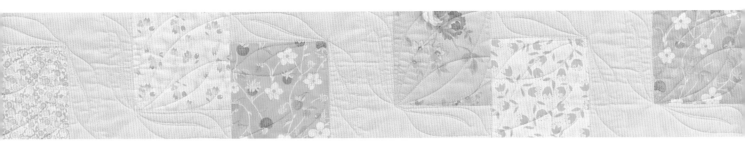

4 Sew three 2½" × 42" border strips together end to end. From the pieced length, cut two strips 42½" long. Trim the remaining two strips to 40½" long. (Before sewing strips together, check the length of the fabric strips after removing selvages. Piecing the strips may not be necessary.)

5 Sew the 42½"-long strips to the sides of the quilt top. Sew the 40½" strips to the top and bottom of the quilt center. The quilt top should measure 40½" × 46½".

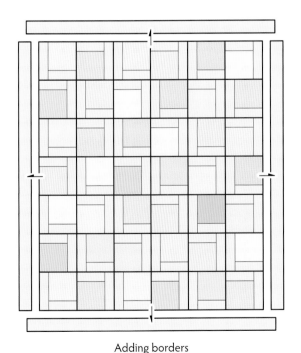

Adding borders

FINISHING

For more help on any of the finishing steps, go to ShopMartingale.com/HowtoQuilt for free downloadable information.

1 Layer and baste the quilt top, batting, and backing fabric.

2 Hand or machine quilt. The quilt shown is machine quilted with overlapping petals in the print squares and with leaves in the background and border.

3 Use the 2¼" strips to make double-fold binding. Trim the excess batting and backing fabric and then attach the binding to the quilt.

Bright, cheerful fabrics, such as Grow by Me and My Sister Designs, almost make the squares look like stacks of festive wrapped gifts.

Black, gray, and white prints from Urban Cottage by Urban Chiks give Quinn a modern look.

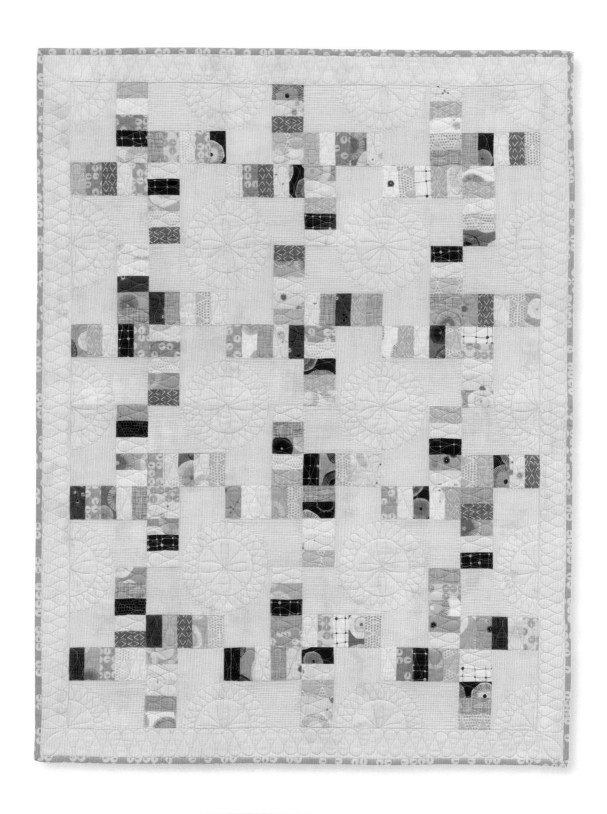

Finished quilt: 34½" × 44½"
Finished block: 5" × 5"

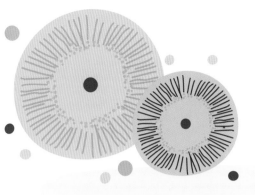

ROXY

If we're allowed to have a favorite, this is it! We were able to lay out this super simple quilt on the kitchen island and have it sewn together before dinner. It has the look of pinwheels with no triangles, and the background areas offer negative space to include some stunning quilting designs.

MATERIALS

Yardage is based on 42"-wide fabric. Fabrics are from Day in Paris by Zen Chic for Moda Fabrics.

- 40 charm squares, 5" × 5", of assorted prints for blocks*
- 1⅛ yards of solid fabric for blocks and border
- ⅜ yard of fabric for binding
- 2⅞ yards of fabric for backing**
- 41" × 51" piece of batting

*Moda charm packs contain 42 squares, 5" × 5".

**If your fabric is at least 42" wide, 1½ yards will be enough.

CUTTING

Refer to the cutting guide for charm squares below.

From *each* charm square, cut:

6 rectangles, 1½" × 2½"

From the solid fabric, cut:

7 strips, 3½" × 42"; crosscut into
  48 rectangles, 3½" × 5½"

2 strips, 2½" × 34½"

2 strips, 2½" × 40½"

From the binding fabric, cut:

5 strips, 2¼" × 42"

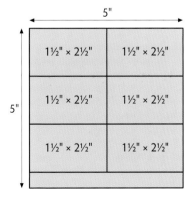

Cutting guide

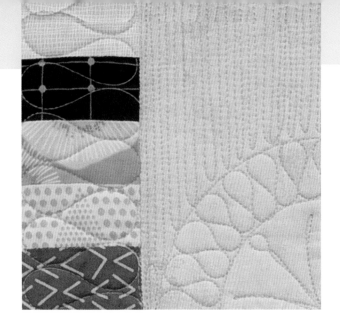

ASSEMBLING THE QUILT

1 Arrange six blocks in a row, rotating them as shown. Join the blocks to make a row that measures 5½" × 30½", including seam allowances. Make eight rows.

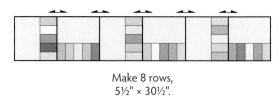

Make 8 rows,
5½" × 30½".

2 Lay out the rows, rotating every other one, so that the rows create a pinwheel design. Join the rows to complete the quilt center, which should measure 30½" × 40½", including seam allowances.

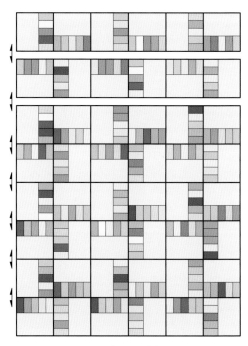

Quilt assembly

MAKING THE BLOCKS

Use a ¼" seam allowance and short stitch length throughout. Press all seam allowances open.

1 For each block, choose the following:
- 5 assorted print 1½" × 2½" rectangles
- 1 solid 3½" × 5½" rectangle

2 Join the five print rectangles as shown to make a unit. Sew this unit to the right side of the solid rectangle to complete a block that measures 5½" square, including seam allowances. Make 48 blocks.

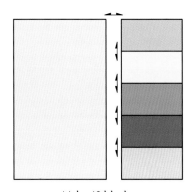

Make 48 blocks,
5½" × 5½".

3 Sew the 40½"-long border strips to the sides of the quilt center. Add the 34½"-long border strips to the top and bottom. The quilt top should measure 34½" × 44½".

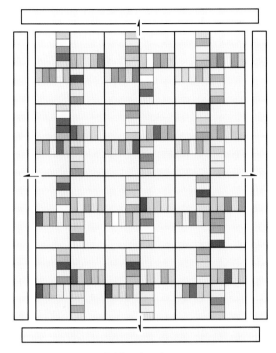

Adding borders

FINISHING

For help with any of the finishing steps, go to ShopMartingale.com/HowtoQuilt for free downloadable information.

1 Layer and baste the quilt top, batting, and backing fabric.

2 Hand or machine quilt. The quilt shown is machine quilted with circular designs and closely spaced continuous lines in the background and with ribbon-candy curves in the border and pieced sections.

3 Use the 2¼" strips to make double-fold binding. Trim the excess batting and backing fabric and then attach the binding to the quilt.

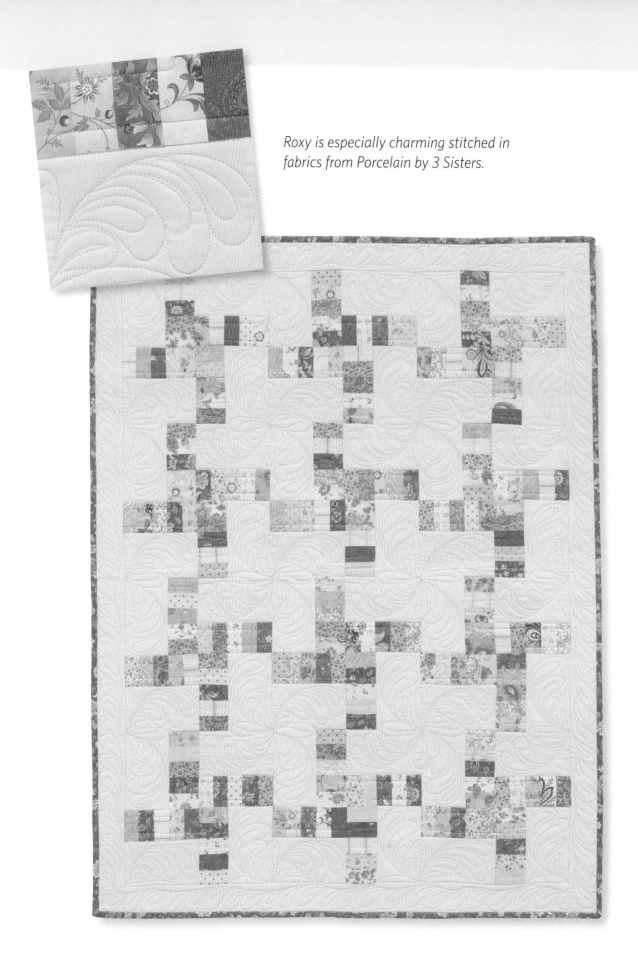

Roxy is especially charming stitched in fabrics from Porcelain by 3 Sisters.

The quilt is happiness itself when sewn with Giggles by Me and My Sister Designs.

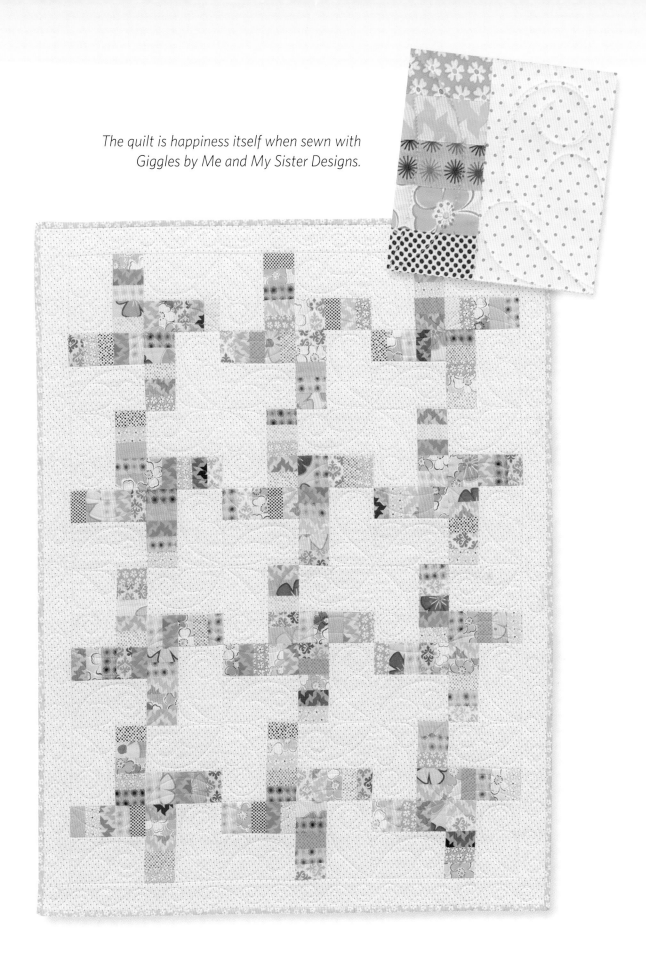

Roxy **29**

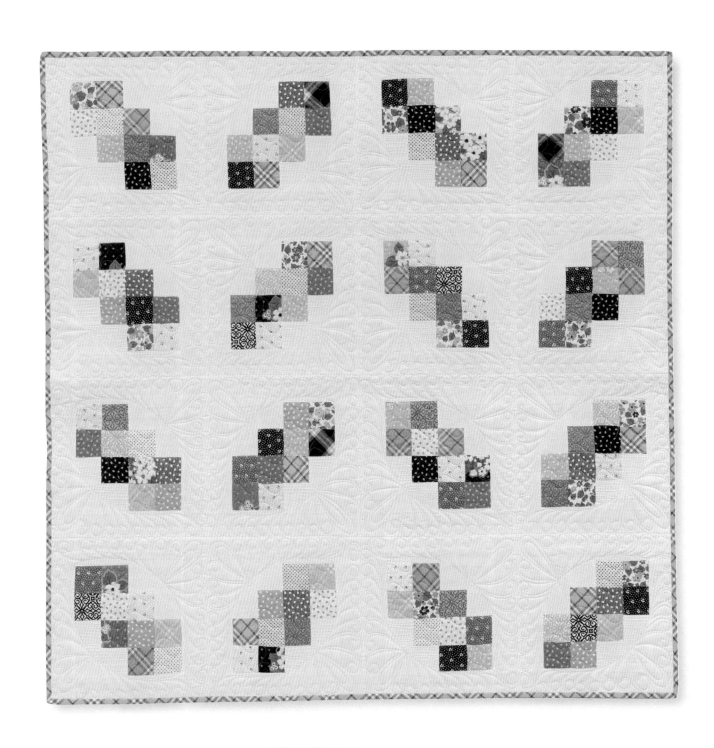

Finished quilt: 48½" × 48½"
Finished block: 12" × 12"

SARAH

Sarah is the largest quilt in the book and is perfect as a lap quilt. It's also an ideal size for a baby quilt, one that can serve for the first few years as the baby grows. All you have to do is cut the charm squares into four squares. The design creates a lot of impact using simple shapes.

MATERIALS

Yardage is based on 42"-wide fabric. Fabrics are from All-Weather Friend by April Rosenthal for Moda Fabrics.

- 40 charm squares, 5" × 5", of assorted prints for blocks*
- 1¾ yards of solid fabric for blocks
- ½ yard of fabric for binding
- 3⅛ yards of fabric for backing
- 55" × 55" piece of batting

*Moda charm packs contain 42 squares, 5" × 5".

CUTTING

Refer to the cutting guide for charm squares below.

From *each* charm square, cut:

4 squares, 2½" × 2½" (160 total)

From the solid for blocks, cut:

2 strips, 2½" × 42"; crosscut into 32 squares, 2½" × 2½"

2 strips, 4½" × 42"; crosscut into 32 rectangles, 2½" × 4½"

2 strips, 8½" × 42"; crosscut into 32 rectangles, 2½" × 8½"

2 strips, 12½" × 42"; crosscut into 32 rectangles, 2½" × 12½"

From the binding fabric, cut:

6 strips, 2¼" × 42"

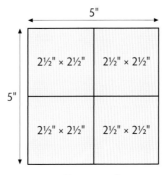

Cutting guide

MAKING THE BLOCKS

Use a ¼" seam allowance and short stitch length throughout. Press all seam allowances open.

1. For each block, choose the following:
   - 10 assorted print 2½" squares
   - 2 solid 2½" squares
   - 2 *each* of the solid 4½", 8½", and 12½" rectangles

2. Lay out all of the squares and two solid 2½" × 4½" rectangles in rows as shown. Join the pieces in each row and then join the rows to make the block center, which should measure 8½" square, including seam allowances.

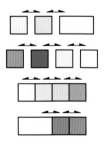

Make 1 unit,
8½" × 8½".

3. Sew the solid 2½" × 8½" rectangles to the top and bottom of the block center. Sew the solid 2½" × 12½" rectangles to the sides to complete the block. Make 16 blocks that measure 12½" square, including seam allowances.

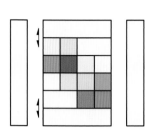 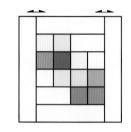

Make 16 blocks,
12½" × 12½".

ASSEMBLING THE QUILT

1. Arrange and sew four blocks together, orienting them so that the diagonal line of prints alternates from block to block as shown. Make four rows. The rows should measure 12½" × 48½", including seam allowances.

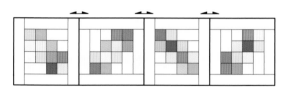

Make 4 rows,
12½" × 48½".

2 Lay out the rows as shown. Sew the rows together to complete the quilt top, which should measure 48½" square.

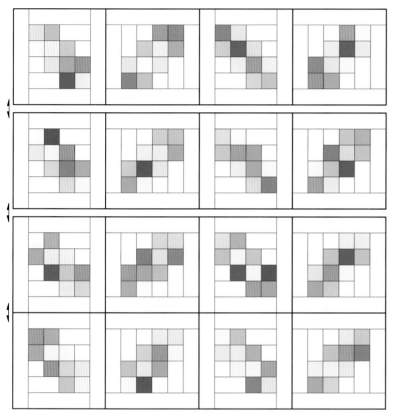

Quilt assembly

FINISHING

For more help on any of the finishing steps, go to ShopMartingale.com/HowtoQuilt for free downloadable information.

1 Layer and baste the quilt top, batting, and backing fabric.

2 Hand or machine quilt. The quilt shown is machine quilted with a feathered oval wreath around the block centers.

3 Use the 2¼" strips to make double-fold binding. Trim the excess batting and backing fabric and then attach the binding to the quilt.

Cheerful fabrics from Ticklish by Me and My Sister Designs create a perky rendition. Note that we set the blocks a little differently in this quilt.

*The orange background and fabrics from
Later Alligator by Sandy Gervais really
let Sarah make a statement.*

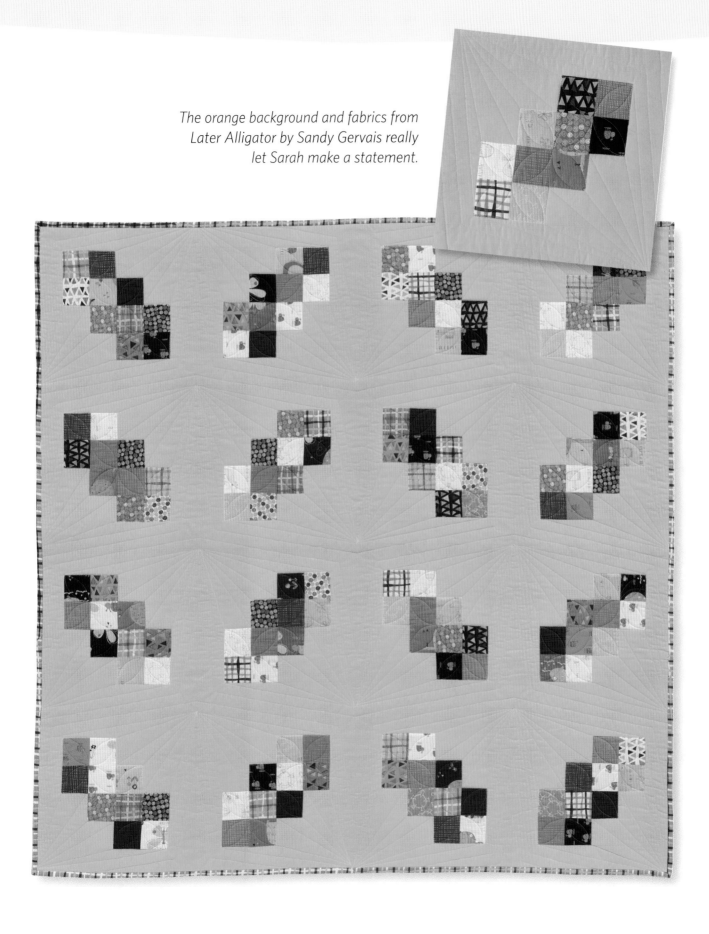

Finished quilt: 24½" × 24½"
Finished block: 4" × 4"

TRACY

Gotta love this girl! She's classic red and white, but hearts lend themselves to any color or print. Choose your favorite colors for a two-color quilt, or use a mixed charm pack for multicolored fun. Do you see rows of hearts, or do you see a zigzag pattern? We see both! Tracy is charming either way.

MATERIALS

Yardage is based on 42"-wide fabric. Fabrics are from Red-iculously in Love by Me and My Sister Designs for Moda Fabrics.

- 36 charm squares, 5" × 5", of assorted prints for blocks*
- ¾ yard of solid fabric for blocks
- ¼ yard of fabric for binding
- ⅞ yard of fabric for backing
- 29" × 29" piece of batting

Moda charm packs contain 42 squares, 5"×5".

CUTTING

Refer to the cutting guide for charm squares below, and keep like prints together.

From *each* charm square, cut:

2 rectangles, 2½" × 4½" (72 total)

From the solid for blocks, cut:

6 strips, 1½" × 42"; crosscut into 144 squares, 1½" × 1½"

5 strips, 2½" × 42"; crosscut into 72 squares, 2½" × 2½"

From the binding fabric, cut:

3 strips, 2¼" × 42"

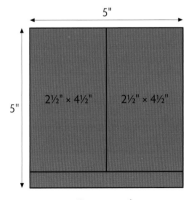

Cutting guide

MAKING THE BLOCKS

Use a ¼" seam allowance and short stitch length throughout. Press all seam allowances open.

1 Draw a diagonal line from corner to corner on the wrong side of the solid 1½" and 2½" squares.

2 For each block, choose:
- 2 matching print 2½" × 4½" rectangles
- 4 solid 1½" squares
- 2 solid 2½" squares

3 With right sides facing, layer a 1½" solid square on the top left corner of a print rectangle. Sew on the marked line. Trim the corner, leaving a ¼" seam allowance. Flip open and press. Repeat on the adjacent side as shown. Make two units that measure 2½" × 4½".

Make 2 units,
2½" × 4½".

4 With right sides facing, layer a solid 2½" square on the bottom of one rectangle, with the diagonal line angled from top left to bottom right. Layer another square on the remaining rectangle, with the diagonal line angled in the opposite direction. Sew on the marked lines, trim the excess corner fabric, leaving a ¼" seam allowance, and press open. The units should measure 2½" × 4½".

Make 1 of each unit,
2½" × 4½".

5 Arrange the two block halves as shown and join to complete a heart block measuring 4½" square, including seam allowances. Make 33 blocks.

Make 33 blocks,
4½" × 4½".

6 Repeat steps 2–4 to make six half blocks that measure 2½" × 4½", including seam allowances.

Make 3 of each half-block,
2½" × 4½".

ASSEMBLING THE QUILT

1. Arrange and sew six blocks to make a row. Make three rows that measure 4½" × 24½", including seam allowances.

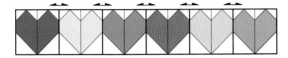

Make 3 rows,
4½" × 24½".

2. Arrange and sew five blocks and two half blocks as shown to make a row. Make three rows that measure 4½" × 24½" including seam allowances.

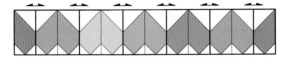

Make 3 rows,
4½" × 24½".

3. Lay out the rows, alternating them as shown. Join the rows to complete the quilt top, which should measure 24½" square.

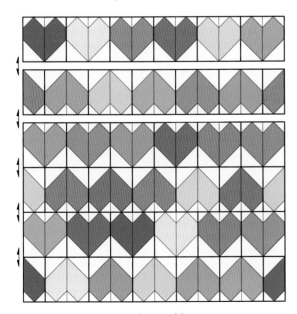

Quilt assembly

FINISHING

For more help on any of the finishing steps, go to ShopMartingale.com/HowtoQuilt for free downloadable information.

1. Layer and baste the quilt top, batting, and backing fabric.

2. Hand or machine quilt. The quilt shown is machine quilted with swirls in the hearts that echo the heart shape. A line of swirls and loops fills the zigzag area.

3. Use the 2¼" strips to make double-fold binding. Trim the excess batting and backing fabric and then attach the binding to the quilt.

We just loved making this quilt with Sweet Harmony by American Jane.

Batiks make beautiful hearts, as evidenced by the Calypso Batiks from Kate Spain.

Finished quilt: 24½" × 24½"
Finished block: 4" × 4"

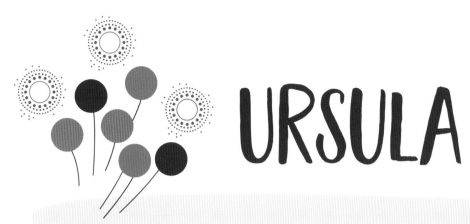

URSULA

We love this scrappy pattern! Try making Ursula larger using four different charm packs from the same designer for an easy and fabulous scrap quilt. Depending on the charm squares and the solids you choose, the quilt can have very different looks. You may even see flowers where four blocks come together.

MATERIALS

Yardage is based on 42"-wide fabric. Fabrics are from Looking Forward by Jen Kingwell for Moda Fabrics.

- 36 charm squares, 5" × 5", of assorted prints for blocks*
- ⅓ yard of solid A for blocks**
- ¼ yard of contrasting solid B for blocks
- ¼ yard of fabric for binding
- ⅞ yard of fabric for backing
- 29" × 29" piece of batting

Moda charm packs contain 42 squares, 5"×5".

**This fabric appears on two corners of the block and creates more of a background; the contrasting solid is added to one corner of the block and creates the more prominent squares when blocks are joined.*

CUTTING

From solid A, cut:
4 strips, 2" × 42"; crosscut into 72 squares, 2" × 2"

From solid B, cut:
2 strips, 2" × 42"; crosscut into 36 squares, 2" × 2"

From the binding fabric, cut:
3 strips, 2¼" × 42"

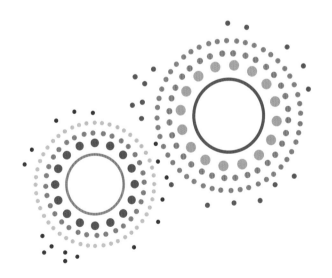

MAKING THE BLOCKS

Use a ¼" seam allowance and short stitch length throughout. Press all seam allowances open.

1 Draw a diagonal line from corner to corner on the wrong side of 18 of the 5" charm squares.

2 Pair a marked square with an unmarked charm square and place them right sides together. Stitch ¼" from each side of the marked line. Cut on the line and press open. Trim the completed half-square-triangle units to 4½" square. Make 36 units.

  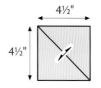

4½"

4½"

Make 36 units.

3 Draw a diagonal line from corner to corner on the wrong side of the 72 solid A squares and 36 solid B squares.

4 With right sides facing, layer two solid A squares on opposite corners of the half-square-triangle unit so that the diagonal lines are parallel to the seam. Stitch on the marked lines, then trim the excess corner fabric, leaving a ¼" seam allowance. Flip open and press to make a unit that measures 4½" square.

Make 36 blocks,
4½" × 4½".

5 Layer a solid B square on one of the remaining corners of the unit. Sew, trim, and press to complete the block, which should measure 4½" × 4½", including seam allowances. Make 36 blocks.

Make 36 blocks,
4½" × 4½".

ASSEMBLING THE QUILT

1 Join six blocks to make a row, alternating the diagonal seam as shown. Make six rows, each measuring 4½" × 24½", including the seam allowances.

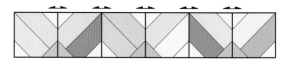

Make 6 rows,
4½" × 24½".

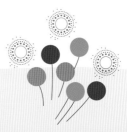

PIN FOR PRECISION

Use pins to match the seams when joining the blocks into rows and when joining the rows. This will ensure that the seams will meet perfectly and that you'll be pleased with the results!

2 Lay out the rows, rotating every other row so that the B solids in the corners create squares in the design. Sew the rows together to complete the quilt top, which should measure 24½" × 24½".

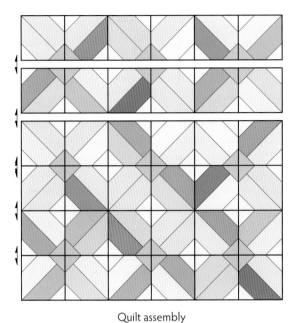

Quilt assembly

FINISHING

For more help on any of the finishing steps, go to ShopMartingale.com/HowtoQuilt for free downloadable information.

1 Layer and baste the quilt top, batting, and backing fabric.

2 Hand or machine quilt. The quilt shown is machine quilted with ribbon candy loops in the prints and a floral design in the solid squares.

3 Use the 2¼" strips to make double-fold binding. Trim the excess batting and backing fabric and then attach the binding to the quilt.

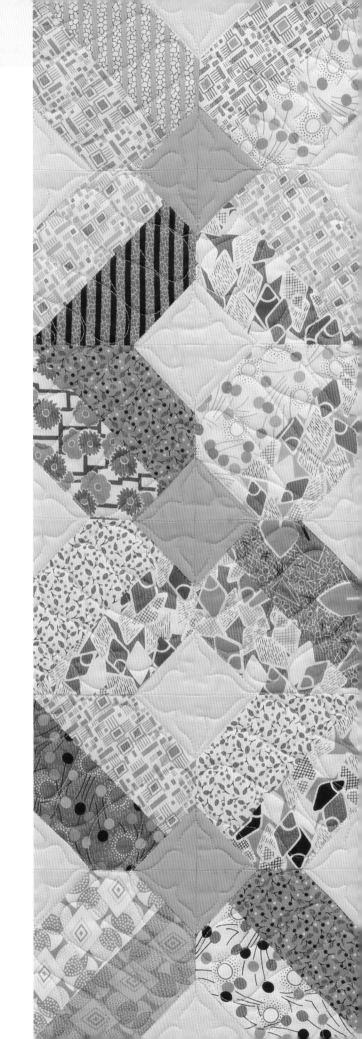

Ursula made in Spring Fever by Me and My Sister Designs is a sure cure for cabin fever.

Walkabout fabrics by Sherri and Chelsi include values from dark to light, giving the quilt extra depth and interest.

ACKNOWLEDGMENTS

The very talented Sharon Elsberry, whose business is called Akamai Quilts, machine quilted all the quilts in this book.

ABOUT THE AUTHORS

Sisters Barbara Groves and Mary Jacobson make up the popular design team of Me and My Sister Designs, based in Tempe, Arizona. Their belief in fast, fun, and easy designs can be seen in the quilts created for their pattern company, in their books, and in their fabric designs for Moda. To learn more, visit the authors at MeandMySisterDesigns.com.